LETTERS

AND

FEELINGS

COLOR THE <u>A'S</u>

A

A M A Z E

ATE

ART

AUNT

ARM

A

A

HOW MANY <u>ARROWS</u> DO YOU SEE? _____

Picture Day!!

Talk to your family about the word <u>Amaze</u>.

Can you draw a picture of a time you were <u>Amazed?</u>

This world is a great place. Try to find something that <u>Amazes</u> you every day.

COLOR THE B'S

BREAD

BALL

BED

BAD

BANANA

HOW MANY BEARS
DO YOU SEE? _____

Picture Day!!

Talk to your family
about the word <u>Bad</u>.

Can you draw
a picture of a time
you felt <u>Bad</u>?

**It is ok to feel <u>Bad </u>sometimes.
It is about what we do to feel
better that matters.**

COLOR THE C'S

CHAIR

CHIN

COAT

CRY

CIRCLE

HOW MANY CATS
DO YOU SEE?

Picture Day!!

Talk to your family about the word <u>Cry</u>.

Can you draw a picture of a time you <u>Cried</u>?

It is ok to <u>Cry</u> sometimes. Always know a safe person who can help you when you <u>Cry</u>.

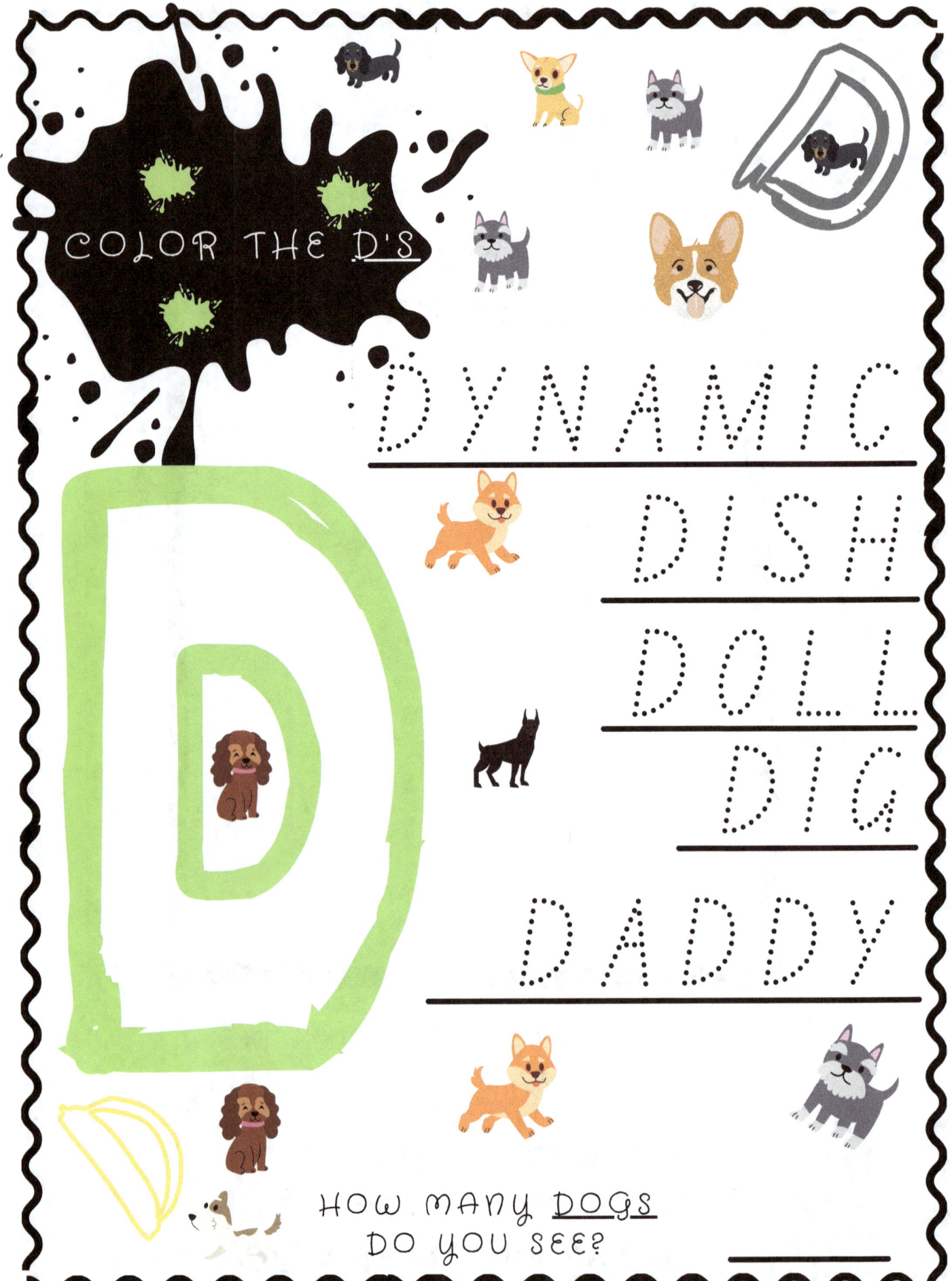

COLOR THE D'S

DYNAMIC

DISH

DOLL

DIG

DADDY

HOW MANY DOGS
DO YOU SEE? _____

Picture Day!!

Talk to your family about the word <u>Dynamic</u>

Can you draw a picture about a time you felt <u>Dynamic</u>?

**Life can be <u>Dynamic</u>.
Make friends who want
you to live <u>Dynamically</u>.**

COLOR THE E'S

EAT

EYE

EAR

EXCITED

EACH

HOW MANY EGGS
DO YOU SEE? _____

Picture Day!!

Talk to your family about the word <u>Excited.</u>

Can you draw a picture of a time you were <u>Excited?</u>

**Feeling <u>Excited</u> is great!
Tell your family what you are
<u>Excited</u> about today.**

EXCITED

EXCITED

COLOR THE F'S

FLY

FOUR

FIVE

FISH

FUN

HOW MANY FLOWERS
DO YOU SEE?

Picture Day!!

Lets talk about having <u>Fun</u>.

Can you draw a picture of something <u>Fun?</u>

It's important to have <u>Fun</u> everyday.
Be safe when having <u>Fun</u> with family and friends.

COLOR THE G'S

G

G

GAS

GREEN

GOOD

GIRL

GLASS

HOW MANY GHOSTS
DO YOU SEE? _____

Picture Day!!

Talk to your family about the word <u>Good.</u>

Can you draw a picture of something <u>Good?</u>

Feeling <u>Good</u> is cool. Try to find a chance to feel <u>Good</u> everyday.

COLOR THE H'S

HAT

HELP

HAIR

HOPE

HORSE

HOW MANY HORSES
DO YOU SEE?
_____

Picture Day!!

Talk to your family about the word <u>Hope.</u>

Can you draw a picture of something you <u>Hope</u> for?

Feeling <u>Hope</u> helps the soul. Find something to <u>Hope</u> for everyday.

ITCH

ISLAND

INK

ICKY

IGLOO

HOW MANY ICE CUBES
DO YOU SEE? _____

Picture Day!!

Talk to your family about the word <u>Icky.</u>

Can you draw a picture
of a time you felt <u>Icky?</u>

**Sometimes when we get sick,
we feel <u>Icky.</u>
When this happens, take it
easy and feel better soon.**

J

JOG

JAW

JOY

JOKE

JACKET

HOW MANY JACKETS
DO YOU SEE? _____

Picture Day!!

Talk to your family about the word J<u>oy</u>.

Can you draw a picture of what J<u>oy</u> looks like?

J<u>oy</u> is the best feeling you can have. What is something you do to feel J<u>oy</u>?

COLOR THE K'S

K

KITE

KICK

KIND

KING

KOALA

HOW MANY KITES
DO YOU SEE?
_____

Picture Day!!

Do you know what it means to be <u>Kind</u>?

Can you draw a picture of a time you were <u>Kind?</u>

<u>Kindness</u> to each other is so important. Can you think of someone who was recently <u>Kind</u> to you?

COLOR THE L'S

LIKE

LICK

LEG

LION

LAUGH

HOW MANY LEAVES DO YOU SEE?

Picture Day!!

Can you name something
that made you <u>Laugh</u>?

Can you draw a picture
of a time you <u>Laughed</u>
the most?

**<u>Laughing</u> can be a sign of happiness.
Celebrate the moments
that make you <u>Laugh.</u>**

MAN

MILK

MIND

MAD

MOMMY

HOW MANY MOONS
DO YOU SEE? _____

Picture Day!!

Have you ever felt Mad?

Can you draw a
picture of a Mad face?

**It's ok to get Mad sometimes.
Just make sure you don't
stay Mad. Whatever or whoever
upset you, work through it.**

COLOR THE N'S

NEAR
NICE
NEW
NAIL
NIGHT

HOW MANY NINES
DO YOU SEE? _____

Picture Day!!

It feels good to
do something <u>Nice</u>, right?

Can you draw a picture of something
<u>Nice</u> someone did for you?

**<u>Nice</u> acts toward others are great.
If you haven't yet, what is something
<u>Nice</u> you could do for your family,
today?**

COLOR THE O'S

ORANGE

OPEN

OUT

OAT

OUCH

HOW MANY OWLS
DO YOU SEE? _____

Picture Day!!

We all get boo boo's that make us say <u>Ouch.</u>

Can you draw a picture of a time you said <u>Ouch?</u>

**When we stumble and say <u>Ouch</u>, it's ok.
Just get back up, dust yourself off and keep on trying,**

COLOR THE P'S

PET

PAL

PIT

PROUD

PROMISE

HOW MANY PIGS
DO YOU SEE? _____

Picture Day!!

Talk to your family about being <u>Proud.</u>

Now that you know what it is, can you draw a picture of a time you felt <u>Proud?</u>

Feel <u>Proud</u> of yourself always. As long as you tried your best and gave it your all, be <u>Proud</u> that you are your best you.

COLOR THE Q'S

QUICK

QUILT

QUEST

QUIET

QUARTER

HOW MANY QUEENS
DO YOU SEE? _____

Picture Day!!

Was there ever a time you had to be <u>Quiet</u>?

Can you draw a
picture of <u>Quiet</u> time?

**<u>Quiet</u> time can be a great time
to think about the day.
It can also be a great time to relax.**

COLOR THE R'S

RAIN

RIGHT

RELAX

RIB

RACE

HOW MANY RABBITS
DO YOU SEE?

_____

Picture Day!!

Have you ever <u>Relaxed</u>?

Can you draw a picture of something you do to <u>Relax.</u>

<u>Relaxing</u> is a great activity. Take a few minutes to <u>Relax</u> everyday to help bring the day to a close.

COLOR THE S'S

SAME

SAIL

SALE

SNAKE

SAD

HOW MANY
SMILEY FACES
DO YOU SEE?

Picture Day!!

Have you ever felt <u>Sad?</u>

Can you draw
a picture of a <u>Sad</u> face?

**It's ok to get <u>Sad</u> sometimes.
When you are <u>Sad</u>, talk to
someone you trust to help you.**

COLOR THE T'S

TOYS

TICK

TRACE

TEN

TIRED

HOW MANY TIGERS
DO YOU SEE? _____

Picture Day!!

Have you ever felt Tired?

Can you draw a picture of what you do when your Tired?

Whenever you feel Tired, rest. There is nothing wrong with taking a break when you need to.

TIRED

TIRED

COLOR THE U'S

UP

US

USE

UGLY

UNDERWEAR

HOW MANY UNICORNS
DO YOU SEE? _____

Picture Day!!

Talk to your family
about the word <u>Ugly</u>.

Can you draw a picture of a time you
might have been <u>Ugly</u>
to someone?

**Know that you aren't <u>Ugly</u> and if you
ever act that way, say your sorry and
make a new friend.**

COLOR THE V'S

VAN

VINE

VASE

VEST

VIBES

HOW MANY VIOLINS
DO YOU SEE?

Picture Day!!

Talk to your
family about <u>Vibes</u>.

Can you draw a picture of
different types of <u>Vibes?</u>

**<u>Vibes</u> help us to read each experience.
Always listen to your <u>Vibes.</u>
They will help you to know if you
are safe.**

COLOR THE W'S

WON

WIG

WIN

WHEN

WORRY

HOW MANY WALRUSES DO YOU SEE? _____

Picture Day!!

Have you ever been Worried?

Can you draw a picture of something that made you Worry?

We all Worry about things. It is ok to Worry but don't let it stop you from enjoying the good things around you.

COLOR THE X'S

X

X - RAY

XAVIER

XYLOPHONE

HOW MANY
XYLOPHONES
DO YOU SEE?

_____

Picture Day!!

Talk to your
family about <u>X-ray.</u>

Can you draw a picture of what
you might see on an
<u>X-ray?</u>

**X is a hard letter for an emotional word.
However, using an <u>X-ray</u> you can
see the truth about what is inside.**

COLOR THE Y'S

YUM

YOU

YES

YUCKY

YELLOW

HOW MANY YAKS
DO YOU SEE?
_____

Picture Day!!

Have you ever touched something <u>Yucky?</u>

Can you draw a
picture of a <u>Yucky</u> face?

**Sometimes you might touch
something <u>Yucky</u>.
If you do, scream "EW" and wash
your hands to get rid of <u>Yuck's</u>.**

COLOR THE Z'S

Z

ZIG
_____

ZEN
_____

ZOO
_____

ZOOM
_____

ZERO
_____

HOW MANY ZEBRAS
DO YOU SEE? _____

Picture Day!!

Talk to your family about the word <u>Zen</u>.

Can you draw a picture of a <u>Zen</u> face?

Feeling <u>Zen</u> is good because it means you feel at peace. Enjoy and share moments of <u>Zen</u> with your family.

4   6

HUNTING

AND

19   NUMBERS   15

WITH YOUR PARENTS HELP
-
LOOK AROUND YOUR HOME
AND LETS HAVE A
SCAVENGER HUNT!!!!

 1

 10

CAN YOU FIND:
ONE <u>DOOR</u>?

CAN YOU FIND:
TWO <u>SHOES</u>?

CAN YOU FIND:
FOUR PILLOWS?

CAN YOU FIND:
SIX <u>B O O K S</u>?

CAN YOU FIND:
SEVEN TOWELS?

CAN YOU FIND:
NINE <u>TOYS</u>?

CAN YOU FIND:
TEN FORKS?

CAN YOU FIND:
ELEVEN
MARKERS?

CAN YOU FIND:
TWELVE <u>SPOONS</u>?

CAN YOU FIND:
THIRTEEN PICTURES?

CAN YOU FIND:
FOURTEEN SHIRTS?

CAN YOU FIND:
SIXTEEN ICE CUBES?

16

CAN YOU FIND:
SEVENTEEN <u>FLOWERS</u>?

CAN YOU FIND:
TWENTY PIECES OF CANDY?

20

Letters, Numbers, & Feelings Oh My

Glo Rose Books